*For both personal or small group study*

# Beauty, Strength, & Power

## A guidebook to empower women

## Melodi Lein

© Copyright 2018 by Melodi Lein

All rights are reserved. No part of this book should be reproduced or transmitted in any form or by any means, electronic or mechanical, including photocopying, recording or by any information storage and retrieval system without written permission from the publisher.

The opinions in this book are the author's and do not necessarily reflect those of the publisher.

7710-T Cherry Park Dr., Ste 224
Houston, Texas 77095
(713) 766-4271

ISBN: 978-1684115891

# Contents

Foreword ................................................................. v
Dedication ............................................................. vii
Acknowledgements ................................................ ix
Endorsements ......................................................... xi
Introduction His Plan for My life ............................ 1
Chapter 1: Beauty Within ......................................... 5
Chapter 2: Understanding My Identity ................... 13
Chapter 3: Heritage ................................................ 19
Chapter 4: Stories Behind Scars ............................. 27
Chapter 5: Greatest Love Story .............................. 35
Chapter 6: Amour de ma vie (Love of My Life) ..... 43
Chapter 7: A Man's Point of View .......................... 51
Chapter 8: Breaking the Curse ................................ 59
Chapter 9: Tears Turned into Dancing .................... 65
Chapter 10: Gift of Motherhood ............................. 73
Chapter 11: Precious Cargo .................................... 79
Chapter 12: Construct Your Future ......................... 87
Grand Finale (Bonus Chapter) ................................ 93
Contact the Author ................................................. 91

# Foreword

"A wife of noble character who can find?" This is a biblical expression which many Christians remember. "Look for them now," some shout, "we urgently need them!"

In a decadent, sick and forgotten world of God we need those strong women (and men). A woman is more than a simple receptacle of divine grace. We have been created to express the glory and greatness of God. Throughout history strong and determined women rose to fulfill God's purpose in their lives. If the presence of the woman had not been necessary, God would not have taken us out of that 'little rib' of man; and in the world there would have been only men. But that was not God's plan. God sent Jesus Christ to dignify the woman and made her enter the main hall of history. Jesus gives the woman the courage that no one gives us in this world. Although it has not been easy to fulfill the role of a woman, it is possible to achieve it when we live completely under the teachings of Jesus Christ and we experience that we no longer depend on our own strength, but on the strength and support that comes from Him. How different a woman is when she lives under the gentle touch of Jesus as she will never be abandoned or despised. Now is the time when God is speaking to women to take their rightful place in the home, church and society. Now is the time that women should develop an effective leadership that is at the forefront to impact the world. I thank God for Melodi Lein and this precious book. She is part of a family with strong Christian values about family. Thank you, Melodi, for this literary work that will bless thousands of women in different stages of their lives. I welcome this book that will help make beautiful and attractive women also be strong and determined in the face of the challenges of the 21st century.

    Noemi L. Mottesi

*"You will be a crown of splendor in the Lord's hand, a royal diadem in the hand of your God."* Isaiah 62:3

# Dedication

I dedicate my book "Beauty Strength and Power" to my parents Daniel and Susana Torres. My three amazing siblings.

My lovely parents-in-law, Henry and Jeannie Lein.

To my husband Jonathan David Lein for being my best friend and number one supporter. To my lovely two sons, Levi Maverick and Liam Nixon Lein for being my inspiration.

I also would like to dedicate this book to every woman reading these pages, seeking God's will for their life.

# Acknowledgments

I thank God for the opportunity to write this book. I thank my mother-in-law and pastor, Jeannie Lein for guiding and motivating me to give women a message of hope and encouragement. I thank evangelist Noemi L. Mottesi, a wonderful woman of God, for her contribution to this book. I would like to thank an amazing friend and pastor Lorena Castellanos for her motivation to my life. Special thanks to my sister and friend Lorena Weg for sharing her powerful story with us and editing each chapter. Last but not least my beloved husband Jonathan for contributing and motivating to write this book.

# Endorsements

In this book, I can see Melodi's heart for women. She has experienced what having an encounter with God means, and how that can change everything. Her experiences in the ministry and in loving people have taken her to have a deeper understanding of compassion. I pray this book takes you closer to God.

*Lorena Castellanos* - MCI Pastor and Music Director for Generación 12 and G12 Worship


'It amazes me how Melodi was able to communicate in such a beautiful way, topics of profound effect in people's lives. This is a delightful book filled with life experiences that remind us all of the beauty, strength and power within our soul. Every woman should read these pages!

*Jeannie Lein* - Senior Pastor at Evermore Church and Founder of Braveheart Movement

# Introduction
## His Plan for My life

Growing up, I seemed to wrestle constantly with knowing God's will for my life. I wanted to follow His plan more than anything, but I have learned that one may struggle with this very issue early in life. Although it is a lifelong pursuit, and I still strive to follow His leadership, I have found the confidence needed in His guiding hand.

Throughout our lives, we are called to make decisions. Should I move here or there? Which college should I go to? Whom should I marry? Should I have kids? The list goes on and on, the longer we live, the more important and life-altering those questions become.

It can be difficult to hear God's voice and know which road to take. We pray and ask God for help, but there are often no signs, no visions, nor strong feelings leading us to the right answer. So how do we know which decision to make, and which road to take?

In Colossians 3:23 (NIV) we read: *And whatever you do, do it heartily, as to the Lord and not to men.* This is an important point. It isn't always what we are to do, but why and how we are to do it. Are we doing it wholeheartedly because we want to please God? Or are we making decisions based on selfish reasons?

It also says in Matthew 7:7 (NIV): *Ask, and it will be given to you; seek, and you will find; knock, and it will be opened to you.* God wants us to seek out for His perfect plan, and He will show us His blueprints if we are willing to follow them. He has promised to be found and to respond to our prayers. His will may not always be what we expect, but know this, His plans are greater than ours.

The Bible makes it clear that there is a perfect plan for each of us. There is proof all around us. The most compelling evidence is that which is written in Scripture: *But the plans of the Lord stand firm forever, the purposes of his heart through all generations.* Psalm 33:11 (NIV).

If we want to know God's plan for our lives, we must walk with Him, and cultivate our relationship with Him. We should seek to know Him for who He is, and not solely for His blessings.

To develop a deeper relationship with God, we must spend quality time in His Word. We must also make time for prayer, and take every opportunity to be involved with our churches. When we seek Him through these spiritual disciplines, He will reveal His plans to us. The wisest thing we can do is to inquire of the Lord about each important decision we make. As we do it, He would see our heart-felt dependency upon Him instead of leaning on our own understanding.

*Trust in the Lord with all your heart and lean not on your own understanding; in all your ways acknowledge Him, and He shall direct your paths.* Proverbs 3:5-6 (NIV)

## Chapter 1:
# Beauty Within

*I praise you because I am fearfully and wonderfully made;
your works are wonderful, I know that full well.*

(Psalm 139:14)

## Beauty, Strength, & Power

**A**s early as I can remember I have always been interested in keeping up a good outer appearance. I've often focused so much on my image that I neglected other areas of my life. I became so worried about the latest trends, fitness goals, make-up tendencies, etc. This mindset wasn't something I was born with, but something taught to me since I was a little girl. Many times, I felt insecure because when comparing myself to those beautiful women in the magazines, I realized, I was never going to look like them. At one point, I broke through society's narrow prototype of beauty and began to love myself the way I am.

Did you know that beauty is not as much about how you look, as it is about how you feel? If you find yourself constantly criticizing something about yourself, whether it's your personality or appearance, this book is for you. Maybe you feel like your hips are too big, or your nose is too long, or you are too old to attract what you desire. Perhaps you dream of the perfect relationship, but feel like you are not pretty enough, smart enough, or young enough. All of that can change when you embrace your inner beauty!

Society sets a narrowly-focused standard of beauty that is virtually impossible for most of us to achieve. So why do we buy into it? When we think about no two faces being the same, how much sense does it make for us to believe that we should look like someone else? Isn't it time we women start loving what makes us unique individuals instead of the pain and suffering that comes from trying to meet someone

## Chapter 1: Beauty Within

else's definition of beauty?

You've heard many times that it is inner beauty that counts. But I assure you it is absolutely true. People, who understand this concept, understand that the soul of a woman is what makes her beautiful. When we strip away everything applied to the outside (the hair extensions, makeup, and push up wardrobes) and we get to the heart of the matter, what truly matters is the heart. That is where true beauty is revealed. We should realize that what we do, in our everyday life and how we care for others would determine the measurement of our true beauty. The Bible reminds us of this in 1 Peter 3:3-4, (NIV) where we read:

*Your beauty should not come from outward adornments, such as braided hair and the wearing of gold jewelry and fine clothes. Instead, it should be that of your inner self, the unfading beauty of a gentle and quiet spirit, which is of great worth in God's sight.*

They are five important points that will certainly make a person beautiful from the inside-out.

**1.  Passion for Jesus.**

Passionate people are the happiest people. They have figured out what drives them in life, and they care enough to pursue their goals. When Jesus becomes your priority, you can't help but be Spirit-filled and full of joy. His love not only fills every void in your heart, but He gives you the confidence to overcome every obstacle. You light up every room you walk into! To be pas- sionate for Jesus gives you real purpose in life.

**2. Compassion for Others.**

It has been said that "Beauty is in the eye of the beholder," and someone who cares more about others than themselves, is a beautiful person. This isn't easy. Compassion never is. But it is a sign of true beauty. When you can look past people's faults, and relate to them on a deeper level, you communicate to them that they are understood.

**3. Intelligence.**

Smart is beautiful. When a person can hold a conversation, debate, or express their own opinions, not having the need to rely on superficial things to make themselves look better, then that person is beautiful. Your words and thoughts speak more about you than any cute little dress or adorable accessory you might purchase. Words have power, and a person who chooses their words wisely expresses inner beauty within minutes of a first impression.

A woman with mixed up priorities only worries about her makeup and hair being fixed at all times, but a fearless women deals with whatever life throws at her. Constantly having to be dolled up is difficult to maintain, but what you carry inside of you, is what really makes you shine. We should always be smiling at the possibility of our next adventure rather than fearing imperfections others may see in us.

**4.     Perseverance.**

Amid tragedy or defeat, a person who places their trust in God will rise above these situations and this is beautiful. The impact of your perseverance will inspire others to trust God, to refuse to quit, and to try again when tragedy strikes. They will see God reflected in your confidence and self-assurance, knowing that you are not afraid to fail. Beauty isn't about being perfect –it's about rising above life's challenges and becoming the strong woman you are meant to be--.

**5.     Personal health care.**

Every woman desires perfect skin, perfect nails, and perfect hair. But how can we obtain them? While many women look for expensive shampoos, the latest beauty products, and salon trips, these can easily be found in our daily meals. We have all heard, "You are what you eat" Right? This statement is true. Eating a healthy, well-balanced diet is the best solution when looking to improve one's appearance. We can even use some natural foods as beauty treatments without consuming them!

Your health is the backbone of long-lasting beauty. Inner transformation will affect your outer beauty by improving the health of your skin, transforming the shape of your body, and al- lowing you to express a radiance that will inspire those around you.

## Beauty, Strength, & Power

I currently have an active Instagram account *@Melsbeautytips* where I emphasize how to enhance our natural beauty. This account was not created to simply talk about the latest beauty tips, but to encourage and empower women around the globe to become women of beauty, strength, and power. In addition, we want to remind everyone that the Creator of the universe formed us with His best ingredients. We are not all cookie-cutter beings! We are each hand-crafted, wonderfully unique, and beautifully made.

Frankly, as a society, our relationship with beauty is in crisis. We are being told that beauty exists only in certain shapes, ages, and sizes. It's easy to feel bombarded with images that lead us away from God's purpose for our lives, and our own unique beauty. Men can be affected by such messages, but women even more so, especially when they desperately want to be loved, approved, considered special, and seen as beautiful.

Remember, God created you in His perfect image. You are His masterpiece! God made you, His princess, full of beauty from the inside out. Everything about you is created to serve His purpose. When you realize your own value, others will accept it and value you as well.

*Chapter 1: Beauty Within*

# Let's Reflect!

1. What area concerning your outer appearance do you struggle with?

   _____

   _____

   _____

   _____

2. Finish this sentence.

   I_____(Your full name) believe I am truly beautiful. I will no longer believe the voices that tell me otherwise. Today___ (Date) I decide to accept myself as I am. I will  never again allow society, friends/family, nor myself to criticize me. God loves me as I am and that is enough. I am___ (Age) year's old, I weight around.___ lbs. And I look good! I do not  need to prove myself to anybody because He has already approved of me. The Lord, who created me, tells me in Song of Solomon 4:7 (NIV) *You are altogether beautiful, my love; there is no flaw in you.*

# Chapter 2:
# Understanding My Identity

*God created man in his own image; in the image of God he created him.*

Genesis 1:27 (NIV)

Have you ever struggled with the question, "Who am I?" Or thought about, who do you might become in the future? These two questions have been pondered and discussed throughout history. We all want to know who we are. Some search many years to find the answers.

First, what is one's identity? It is the concept we develop about ourselves that evolves over the course of our lives. This may include different aspects of it, such as culture, exposure to various beliefs and family. The choices we make in life, how we invest our time, and what we believe certainly help to shape it.

Often, people base their identities on what they do (from their jobs to their roles in relationships). They define themselves by those pursuits. Many of us have taken personality tests and have compared ourselves to others seeking our own unique personal trademark. But by doing so, we significantly limit ourselves. Our identities develop over time and can evolve, sometimes drastically, depending on what have been done to us or what directions we choose to take in life. Perhaps your parents said things to you as a child that made you doubt your worth. Maybe you were rejected or abused. Possibly you are someone who experienced severe rejection and abuse in the past. Memories of that sort build up over time, causing deep wounds, eventually causing us to be self-defensive, even rejecting others.

For years, I struggled with my identity. I felt lost,

## Chapter 2: Understanding My Identity

insecure, and without any sense of direction. I had difficulties with my relationship with God. Although I called myself a Christian, I didn't have a real relationship with Him. I attended church every Sunday and was a "good kid." But I had not found my true identity in Christ. Instead, I created an image based on who my friends were, what activities I was involved with, and how I looked.

Then one day, at the age of 14, I went to my first *Encounter*. There, I experienced the greatest love of all, the love of my Father God. I learned that by getting to know my heavenly Father and Creator, I would comprehend who I was. I discovered that neither my successes nor mistakes defined me, but rather the merciful grace of God upon my life. His forgiveness overwhelmed me, and my heart found everlasting freedom. I finally understood that God created me in His likeness and I was able to find myself in Him. It was in that remarkable moment, that I decided to live my entire life serving the One who gave His all for me.

The truth is that God intends for all people to find their identity in Christ. However, very few take the time to ask, "What does God, my Creator, think of me?" I also understood the power of my words and the consequences for my life. The thoughts we think and the words we speak help define our future—for good or for bad.

How we perceive ourselves drives what we think, say and do; to that cycle, add the influence of other people in our lives, and the power of what they think, say and do about us.

In too many cases, our true selves, created in the image of God, becomes distorted by wrong ideas of the enemy planted in our minds, and other people's concepts. He wants to remind us of our identity in Christ. He wants us to be mindful that we are His masterpiece. He took the time to create every detail about us and he drove us to perfection. Jeremiah 1:5 (NIV) reminds us that He had a plan even before we were created!

*Before I formed you in the womb I knew you, and before you were born I consecrated you; I appointed you a prophet to the nations.*

Our single most valuable, yet least understood possession is our identity in Christ. Our Father designed us to be content. Paul wrote to Timothy, his mentee, that godliness with contentment is great gain. 1 Timothy 6:6(NIV) The more we learn about our *true* identity, the more closely we are drawn to Him.

*See what great love the Father has lavished on us, that we should be called children of God! And that is what we are!*
1 John 3:1-2 NIV)

*Chapter 2: Understanding My Identity*

# Let's Reflect!

1) Without using your name, age, gender or nationality. Who are you?

_____
_____
_____
_____

2) Why did God create you? What is your purpose on earth?

_____
_____
_____
_____

**Prayer.**

*Lord, today I ask you to please reveal your word to me. Through this book, I recognize I need your guidance to make personal, career, and financial decisions. I surrender all my plans and all my dreams to you. I accept the original design you have for my life. Help me hear your voice, teach me to become humble and be obedient to your guidance. I know your plans are higher than mine. So, I surrender fully to you God, in Jesus name I pray. Amen.*

## Chapter 3:

# Heritage

*Can a mother forget the baby at her breast and have no compassion on the child she has borne? Though she may forget, I will not forget you!*

Isaiah 49:15 (NIV)

**L**et me tell you about a story that marked my life a few years ago. One day as I finished preaching at our youth service, a girl came up to me. She was visiting our church for the first time and asked for my name, when I told her; she immediately began to get teary eyes.

I wasn't sure what was going on, until she began to tell me her story. When she was younger, she invested her time in a relationship. One day she found out that she was expecting a baby. Unfortunately, neither her boyfriend nor her family, approved. So, she thought the best solution was to abort her baby. She tried several different ways to abort her child, but each time, she failed. Then she went to a clinic, and in a matter of minutes, they killed her baby in her womb and removed it piece-by-piece. She said that she left that clinic feeling little to no guilt.

A few years later she encountered the love of God, and her life was completely trans- formed. One night, in a dream, God took her on a journey. She said that in her dream, an angel came, took her by the hand, and showed her a specific part of heaven. In that place she saw many joyful children dancing and playing. Then the angel took her near Jesus, who was holding a little girl in His arms. Immediately her heart began to pound. Jesus said, "This is your daughter I am holding, her name is Melody." The darling girl looked into her eyes and said, "Mommy don't cry! I have already forgiven you. I am happy here." God gave this young woman the opportunity to see this special place in heaven where

## Chapter 3: Heritage

unborn and aborted babies had their home.

As she related me her story, my heart was broken, and I could feel what God feels each time a baby dies before its time. And I assure you, the pain was unbearable. I felt as if a huge weight was placed upon my shoulders and a burden for every innocent infant being murdered every second. Did you know that from 2010 - 2014 there was an average of 56 million induced abortions that occurred each year? Please consider that these statistics increase every year. Of course, these are only those abortions that have been reported. What a horrific thought! Millions of babies never got a chance to live. Abortion is the world's easiest alternative for unwanted children. From that point, I decided to do whatever is in my power to bring awareness to the cause of innocent lives.

That is why today I must tell you that abortion is a sin before God. The Bible speaks clearly about the value of unborn children. God's Word says that He personally made each of us with a plan for our lives.

*"For you created my inmost being; you knit me together in my mother's womb. I praise you because I am fearfully and wonderfully made; your works are wonderful, I know that full well. My frame was not hidden from you when I was made in the secret place, when I was woven together in the depths of the earth. Your eyes saw my unformed body; all the days ordained for me were written in your book before one of them came to be"* **Psalm 139:13-16 (NIV).**

Sometimes the circumstances surrounding a pregnancy are tragic. Perhaps the woman was raped. Maybe the baby has been diagnosed with a physical defect. Or the woman's health might be at risk. However, one tragedy is not answered with another. We do not erase a rape by killing a child. We do not cure a baby by taking his life. And we do not avoid all health issues by avoiding the reality of another human being.

A child does not deserve to die for the crimes of his father. A five-year-old should not be killed because his father was a rapist; nor should an unborn child be allowed to be killed for the same reason. A child does not deserve to die because their mother and/or her father were irresponsible. No child decided that his parents would have sex, or that they would use ineffective contraception. An innocent unborn child should never be punished.

No matter how hard we try, we can never erase what abortion does. It kills an innocent human being. Time does not erase a murder or ease the reality of what it is. Abortion is a cruel choice that should never be made. Such a choice stays with us forever.

For anyone who has already participated in an abortion, while there is no way to change your past, there is a way to heal from it. God has given women the most important job, to be fruitful and multiply. To give life, to nourish, to protect, to provide and most importantly to love

## Chapter 3: Heritage

our children. Today I invite you to pray the following prayer with me and ask for forgiveness if you ever declared you would never have children, have aborted your baby, or despised your children.

*"God, I come to you broken and ashamed. I am sick with regret and don't know where else to go. Have mercy on me. I know that the choice I made to end my pregnancy defied your heart and your law. You create life. We must never presume that it is ours to give or take it away.*

*My own life is a gift from you; I would not want another person to determine my destiny. And yet in my desperation, I made that choice. I assumed your role and played God. I took a life in my hands. Yes, I panicked and couldn't see how I would live, let alone raise up a child.*

*But there is hope for me. Father God, today I ask for forgiveness for every thought against your will. For every harm to myself and my future generation. I repent of all sin; I invite Jesus into my heart. Lord restore me and make me new. I declare that you, God, has extended your mercy toward me and have given me forgiveness, protection, grace, honor, and peace. Amen."*

# Let's Reflect!

1. Have you or someone you know attempted or committed an abortion? If yes, who, and when? If multiple people, please make a list.

_____

_____

_____

_____

    Whether you're contemplating an abortion, or are living through the post-abortion experience, please reach out to a trusted mature Christian mentor who will walk alongside you on this admittedly confusing journey. You don't have to face this alone. Make an appointment with your pastor. If they don't feel equipped to do so, ask them to recommend someone. There are ministries which focus is on helping people just like you. Please know it is 100% confidential.

    I pray that as you have read this chapter, the Lord has revealed to you the spiritual dimensions of abortion and unwanted pregnancies and that He may place in your heart a burden for those innocent lives.

*Chapter 3: Heritage*

*Lord God, forgive our nation for each child's life that has been taken. Use each of us to bring reconciliation between these women and You. Allow us to be part of the movement to stop legalized abortions. In Jesus name, Amen.*

## Chapter 4:
# Stories Behind Scars

*He heals the brokenhearted and binds up their wounds.*

Psalm 147:3(NIV)

I want to tell you a story of someone whom I love very much, someone who experienced restoration first hand. I know that her testimony will minister to you. The following is her amazing story

**She wrote...**

If someone had told me that this would be my story, I would have never believed it, not in a million years!

*"Sing, barren woman, you who never bore a child; burst into song, shout for joy, you were never in labor; because more are the children of the desolate woman than of her who has a husband," says the Lord. "do not be afraid; you will not be put to shame. Do not fear disgrace; you will not be humiliated. You will forget the shame of your youth and remember no more the reproach of your widowhood. 6 The Lord will call you back as if you were deserted and distressed in spirit. A wife who married young, only to be rejected,' says your God"* Isaiah 54:1-6.

She was only five-years-old when she gave her life to Christ, after witnessing a marvelous miracle. From that time on, she was privileged to grow up in a wonderful church, surrounded by a loving family, and with friends who loved the Lord. As a young girl, she dreamed about her prince, a white dress, and a beautiful fairytale marriage although the most important thing to her was praying to remain in the center of the perfect will of God.

Years went by and she met someone in church who

## Chapter 4: Stories Behind Scars

met all the criteria; hers, her parents, her pastors, and even her friends. He promised to be "the one." so they waited, prayed and fasted and soon came the time to walked down the aisle at age 22. She honestly thought her dreams were coming true.

After three short months of paradise, everything drastically changed. They were offered the opportunity to develop a branch of the family business that would require them to move to a distant city, (1,250 miles away) in another country. Their honeymoon quickly turned into a frightening experience as everything began to go wrong. They were far away from family and friends. They invested most of their savings in that desolate place. She still believed that love would conquer it all... they could face everything together and come out of trials successfully. After all, they had each other, and their love would keep them safe and strong.

One lonely night, while waiting for her husband to come home from work, she found a note with a rose instead, that said, "I can't fulfill my words to you, go back to your parents, sorry. I will follow you soon." She was crushed, brokenhearted, and stranded alone in a different country. She didn't have the money to go back home to her parents. Finally, she was able to catch a ride on a truck, next to a stranger, all by herself... she felt sad, confused, and defeated. The shame, fear, and humiliation of that experience had left her without words to express how miserable she felt. She was depressed, alone, and isolated. She cried every day and prayed to find an escape from that awful reality. On the other hand, she waited, hoping for a phone call, an apology, or something from her husband that indicated that they could restore their marriage, and recuperate what they have lost. That call came seven months later and they met again only to discover even more hurtful parts to their story, which left nothing else to be saved from their marriage. The walk to the courthouse was the last thing that they would ever do together. That is when she became a deserted and distressed wife who married young, only to be rejected. (Isaiah 54:6) Little did she know that she was about to uncover God's plan for her life, the plan that she had prayed for so long! It was a plan that would still take more than 12 years to unfold...

Meanwhile, she remembers thinking, *"This is wrong, this could never be the will of God! I must have done things wrong, it's impossible."* The blue days seemed endless as she walked through the darkest valley of her life. She experienced different levels of grief, remorse, questioning herself, asking God, and trying to make sense of it all. She was desperate for answers that no one seemed to have. It took her a long time to make peace with it, and to learn how to trust God; even when she did not sense His presence or anything good for her future.

Jesus was there, gently, softly healing her heart, restoring her soul, teaching her how to follow Him even when her plans did not aligned with His. "*Yes,* she said, *I found myself in deeper waters where I could only trust you*

## Chapter 4: Stories Behind Scars

*Lord"*. The most challenging part of her journey was having to deal with the unknown, and the "why".

Then after seven years, God graciously revealed His purpose for her life through His word in Isaiah 54. She finally understood what He had in mind when He created her. *"I will never forget that precious day! I can still feel the warmth of His embrace, the sweetness of His love, His compassion, His never-ending mercy being poured over me like a healing oil, trickling down from the pages of my Bible"* she said. This beautiful chapter of the bible was a heavenly gift that she held in her heart for the next four years as she waited for her promise to materialize.

*"My blessing came around Christmas, when I finally set my eyes on him, -my miracle, - as I call him, the one who would tenderly teach me to trust again..."* she wrote.

Without so many words, and little by little, he showed her the meaning of everlasting, noble, and tangible love. Something real, something beautiful. Their paths intertwined so perfectly together that they knew it was designed by their heavenly Father. That was exactly what it was, God's perfect plan for them, so they decided that they had waited long enough, and said, *"Yes, yes we do."*

Years have passed now, and this chapter from Isaiah has been the foundation of their marriage and their life together. She said "*Our precious son is the living proof of how God, who started the good work in us, is faithful to complete it. (Philippians 1:6) The Lord not only restored my heart, my soul, and my mind from the inside out, but He also made me completely whole again. He has turned my mourning into dancing, my barrenness into fruitfulness! He has made me a mother. Praise His Holy Name! Every area of my life has been touched by the promise of God. He has done as He promised, and so much more..."*

I challenge you to trust Him today, in every area of your life. He cares for you and knows exactly what you need and how to meet every one of them. He is an Awesome God!

Restoration is more than mending our broken hearts and bringing closure to the sad chapters in our lives. It's about finding and fulfilling His purpose for our lives. He makes things new. We can never change the past, but there is a positive way to look at it. Our greatest tragedies mark us, and those scars remain there to tell the world that our God heals and restores the wounded and the broken.

*Chapter 4: Stories Behind Scars*

# Time to reflect!

1. If the scars of your heart could speak, what would they say about you?

   _____
   _____
   _____
   _____

2. What area of your life do you need God to restore?

   _____
   _____
   _____

3. Start your healing process now. Write down the names of the people who hurt you at some point in your life.

   _____
   _____
   _____
   _____

Pray this prayer with me.

*Father God, give me the ability to forgive today. I decide to forgive each one of the people who have hurt me. I've carried this burden too long. I leave it all in your hands. I choose to forgive not because of them, but because you first forgave me. Lord, please heal my broken heart, and teach me not to hold resentment against them. I receive your love right now. By the power of the blood of Jesus Christ, I am healed. In your mighty name, I pray. Amen.*

## Chapter 5:
# Greatest Love Story

*For God so loved the world that he gave his one and only Son, that whoever believes in him shall not perish but have eternal life.* John 3:16 (NIV)

Can I talk to you about my absolute favorite subject? It is the most important, most talked about, and most complicated subject of all time. Yup, you guessed it! It is the topic of *love*. You see, the first thing we must know about it is that love has neither a beginning nor an end. It is not a feeling that comes and goes at the whim of our emotions. If it is in your heart, it will eventually take over every cell in your body. Love changes our brains, the way we move and talk. Love lives in our spirit and graces us with its presence each day.

Unfortunately, through media, we are constantly bombarded with unrealistic expectations. Meanwhile, in real life, our own experiences and perceptions of love are different; we may get involved in poor, hurtful, and short relationships. No matter your age, race, or gender we all struggle with loneliness, often a result of a lack of love.

There are some who never experienced true love, the kind of love that fills the emptiness inside and replaces our tears with overwhelming joy. Sometimes the absence of it can be felt in one's family—their own home. Too often the parental role is perceived only as a provider or authority figure but never of love and affection. If you've ever experienced rejection, deceit, indifference, heartbreak, and abandonment among other things, I invite you to take a peek at finding the true meaning of love.

## Chapter 5: Greatest Love Story

*What is real love?*

In 1 Corinthians 13:4-8 we read,

*"Love is patient, love is kind. It does not envy, it does not boast, it is not proud. It does not dishonor others, it is not self-seeking, it is not easily angered, it keeps no record of wrongs. Love does not delight in evil but rejoices with the truth. It always protects, always trusts, always hopes, always perseveres. Love never fails."*

This kind of love comes from God who loved us first. He is the definition of love and He delights to show us affection. In the same way, He designed it so that we can learn to experience and express love. The earthly love between a husband and wife is to be an echo of the passionate love and fervent pursuit Jesus has for those who believe in Him—His bride. The powerful and deceptive lure of sin has forced a chasm between God and man, turning our affections from our first love, and focusing on the temporary things of this world. This has resulted in emptiness, death, and destruction. (Isaiah 59:2; Romans 3:23)

Here lies the greatest love story. *"This is how God loved the world: He gave his one and only Son, so that everyone who believes in him will not perish but have eternal life"* John 3:16(NIV). And, *"God showed his great love for us by sending Christ to die for us while we were still sinners"* Romans 5:8(NIV).

While it is beautiful to see the love a man and woman

can share for decades, it pales in comparison to the amazing and eternal love that God offers us. That's the greatest love story! You are the object of His deepest affection. It was for you that Jesus came into the world and laid His life. It was for you that He was crucified, buried, and rose again; conquering sin, death, and the grave. And it is for you that He is coming again to take you away. And yes, you will live happily ever after.

So, the next time you hear the words "God loves you," don't think - that's nice -, and continue to walk away unaffected by that truth, living beneath your privileges. Instead, begin to dwell as someone who knows that every promise in the Book belongs to you. Live like you know you are loved by a great, big God who is concerned about you and involved in every detail of your life. Meditate that fundamental truth over and over in your mind until it sinks to the depths of your soul. As you understand His powerful promise, which is that He will always love you and will never abandon you, it will become easy to discover the true meaning of love and your life will be forever changed.

It is beautiful to understand that our God loves us at our lowest. He reaches out even when we have chosen to run away from Him. He takes us back, when our sins condemns us. There is never a place so far away that He won't go for you. The Bible is God's love letter to you and me. From cover to cover He calls out our names. From the table of contents to the maps in the back. God has marked the course

## Chapter 5: Greatest Love Story

of our lives and has answered the questions we were too afraid to voice.

God is writing His endless love story on the tablets of our hearts. Each page is engraved with His invitation to come and be refreshed by His goodness and favor. Every promise is signed with His precious blood, sealed with His perfect love, and delivered as an arrow aimed straight at the target. This great love story is filled with action, passion, intrigue, war, peace, and romance. After all, the unstoppable passion and desire God the Father has for you is *The Greatest Story Ever Told!*

Beauty, Strength, & Power

# **Time to reflect!**

1. Have you ever accepted Jesus into your heart?

   _____

2. If you answered "no," would you like to invite Jesus in your life?

   _____

3. If you answered "yes," would you like to rededicate your life to Jesus once more?

   *Heavenly Father, I recognize that I have not lived my life for You up until now. I've made many mistakes in my life. I need You in my life. I acknowledge the sacrifice of Your Son Jesus Christ in giving His life for me on the cross, and I long to receive the forgiveness you have made freely available to me through this sacrifice.*

   *Come into my life now, Lord. Take up residence in my heart and be my king, my Lord, and my Savior. From this day forward, I will no longer be controlled by sin, or the desire to please myself, but I will follow You.*

*Chapter 5: Greatest Love Story*

*Father please write my name in the book of life and never erase it. I ask this in Jesus' precious and holy name. Amen.*

## Chapter 6:

# Amour de ma vie
# (Love of My Life)

*Let love and faithfulness never leave you; bind them around your neck, write them on the tablet of your heart.*

*Then you will win favor and a good name in the sight of God and man.*

Proverbs 3:3-4 (NIV)

Allow me to share with you, through my eyes; what I believe is vital if we are to find our other half. I have been blessed with my husband Jonathan. Through our lovely and successful marriage, God has blessed us with two sons, Levi and Liam. I believe with all my heart that we are truly soul mates. I am more in love with John today, after our first six years of marriage than ever before. God has been the center of our relationship since day one. Though it hasn't been easy, we constantly consecrate ourselves before God. And even when we go through trials, we have learned to seek the One who put us together in the first place. For every struggle, John and I emerge stronger. It is such a blessing to find someone after God's heart with whom you can spend your life.

Whether you are searching for your future mate, or have found yours, it is important to grasp and appreciate each stage of the relationship, and how to pray and follow God's direction.

As women, we desire to love and be loved. We also dream about a relationship with someone who God has perfectly designed for us. Faith is a key ingredient to finding that person. We must trust God, that He has our special someone out there. For those of us, who have found "the one," we are to fall in love with them more deeply each day.

For some people, there are times when it feels as if true love has passed by, or that the hope of finding a soulmate has vanished. I encourage you to pause and have a

## Chapter 6: Amour de ma vie (Love of My Life)

conversation with God. Tell Him about what you feel, specifically; tell him about your desires and wants.

Unfortunately, when it comes to love and relationships, these days, too many seem to be walking along a bumpy road. There is a chronic love problem in our generation. People are losing touch with love. We must get back to it if we are going to succeed, we must define what is essential about relationships and analyze what is love and what is not. I can simply describe it in a few stages.

*The romantic stage:* everyone loves it! Everything tastes sweet and makes our hearts beat double-time.

*The transition stage:* reality sets in, and we now learn that not everything is as perfect as it seemed when we started.

*The acceptance stage*: we try to make things work and hold things together despite our flaws and failures.

*The commitment stage*: we make a long-term commitment to the other person and dream of the possibility of a family together.

Let's talk about marriage and relationships and how God sees them. In the Bible, God presents His view of marriage. In Matthew 19:4-5 we read, *"Haven't you read," he replied, "that at the beginning the Creator 'made them male and female,' and said, 'For this reason a man will leave his father and mother and be united to his wife, and the two will become one flesh'?*

Notice the original form of marriage set by God. To Him, marriage is only acceptable between one man and one woman.

The Lord has revealed His plan for humanity and His intentions for marriage and sexuality. While Scripture teaches that homosexual acts are sinful, it isn't about condemning homosexuals, gays, lesbians, or transgender people. This topic is controversial, so let me clarify. We Christians do not have the authority to condemn or judge anyone on God's behalf. We are to show love to one another, as God loves us. We are to believe, practice, and teach only what is written in God's Word. We are people who have a fallen nature and live in a fallen world. But in Christ, we can be made new creations.

Sometimes in the search to find a true soulmate, we encounter deception, setbacks, and too often heartbreak. If you have been a victim of unsuccessful relationships, this book was written for you. I know! Trust me, I've been there. I know how it feels to be on that side, wondering if you will ever move on, if God will forgive you, or if it's even possible to find your "Mr. Right." Maybe you've even wondered if God has forgotten about you.

The most perfect love is the love of God. In 1 Corinthians 13:8 we are told that *"love never fails."* The love of God never fails to reach out to a distant person who has grown cold and hard. Love never fails to conquer years of neglect. Love is all-powerful because it never fails.

*Chapter 6: Amour de ma vie (Love of My Life)*

Friend, pray for God to heal your past heartache, repent of all your sins, and for emotional and spiritual deception. Whether married or single, we can be made new, ready for a true and healthy love.

I invite you to pray with me. Ask God to remove your painful memories and heartbreaks from the past. Open your heart to the Holy Spirit. He knows your deepest thoughts, feelings, and desires. I promise He can bring total healing to your life, simply ask Him,

*"Lord, please heal my 'love wounds.' Help me heal from grief, loss, shame, and the pain of lost love in my past. Make me whole and happy again. I have been needy and overly-anxious. I have felt desperate and sometimes too willing to settle for too little. Calm the need in me to make unwise choices.*

*Forgive me, Lord, for I have sinned and defiled my sexuality mentally and (or) physically. Jesus, wash me with your precious blood and make me new again. Soothe the soreness in my soul that makes me crave affection. Restore my faith in true love and divine timing. Bring love to me, at the right time, for the right reasons. Let the healing of my heart begin. Amen!"*

When two loving souls come together, it is a beautiful thing. When you find true love, it's important to value that person, to build the relationship stronger each day.

## Beauty, Strength, & Power

Let's ask the Lord to bless you and your beloved each moment of every day. Ask God to cover you both with protection, carry you through the hard times together, and lead you both to be in His perfect will.

Allow the Lord to rekindle the fire of your love. Pray to be inspired each day to become passionate soulmates and always willing to care about and love each other more each day. If you are married, I invite you to pray this with me.

*Dear Heavenly Father, thank you for our life together, for the gift of love, and the blessing of our marriage. I give you praise for the joy you've poured into our hearts through the love we share. Thank you for the contentment of family, and the happiness of our home. May we always treasure the experience of loving each other in holy union.*

*Help us remain forever committed to the vows we made to each other, and to you, Lord. We need your strength daily as we live together with the goal of following and serving you. Develop within us the character of your Son, Jesus, that we might love each other with the love he demonstrated—with patience, respect, understanding, honesty, forgiveness, and kindness.*

*Let us always support one another, a friend to listen and encourage, a refuge from the storm, and most importantly, a warrior in prayer. In Jesus name, I pray, Amen!*

*Chapter 6: Amour de ma vie (Love of My Life)*

# Time to Reflect!

1. What is the most important prayer request related to your love life?

   _____
   _____
   _____
   _____

2. Would you accept the challenge? Memorize these Bible verses.

*Love is patient, love is kind. It does not envy, it does not boast, it is not proud. It does not dishonor others, it is not self-seeking, it is not easily angered, it keeps no record of wrongs. Love does not delight in evil but rejoices with the truth. It always protects, always trusts, always hopes, always perseveres.* 1 Corinthians 13:4-7 (NIV).

PS: Place them on sticky notes around your house!

# Chapter 7:
# A Man's Point of View
### By John Lein

*Then the Lord God said, "It is not good that the man should be alone; I will make him a helper fit for him"*

Genesis 2:18 (NIV)

## Beauty, Strength, & Power

In this chapter, we will see things from a man's perspective, from my beloved husband John Lein. What does a man truly desire in a woman? John writes:

I always had the desire to be married one day, to find the person that I could call my soul mate. And as I went through life looking for that person, there were many characteristics that I had in mind. But in my search, I realized something both interesting and shocking. What is that you may ask? Well, as you know, guys engage in "locker room talk." Being an interactive person, I always liked to hear what they considered a desirable soul mate. This is what I heard nine times out of ten.

Many guys I listened to bragged about how they did not pursue women, they made women come pursue them. When I heard that I immediately thought, "Yeah that is exactly what not to do." If I see a woman chasing a man, the first thing that comes to mind is that she is desperate. This in most cases means that she is "needy". She is desperate to feel loved, to feel important or significant, so she throws herself at men wanting to feel love, even if it is for a moment. Believe me, wicked men know how to take advantage of women, because all they crave is sex for a one-night stand.

It is unfortunate, through social media men are taught that the more women they are intimate with, the better off they will be. After all, they say, why get married when you can have multiple partners and have zero responsibility. The media continuously feeds us this information to the point

## Chapter 7: A Man's Point of View

that sexual immorality has become normality, and marriage is seen as something strange to our generation.

But I assure you that you do not need to throw yourself at a man. You are unique and a precious treasure. You are valuable and worthy to be protected and respected. And you must also respect yourself. A person with self-respect will wait for God's person and the right time. Among themselves, guys have "terms" for women. They will either say, "That girl is 'wife material.'" Or, they will say, "That girl is 'easy.'" I do not mean to offend you, but that is literally what I have heard guys commonly say. So, here are three points of what a godly man is looking for in his soul mate. As you consider them, ask yourself if you are "wife material," or "easy."

### 1. Does she hold herself to a higher standard?

Another way of saying it, "Does she know who she is. Or does she throw herself at any guy for attention?" A woman who holds herself to a higher standard is more attractive because it is clear that she has a good head on her shoulders, she is not messing around. When she is ready for a significant relationship, she is "wife material."

### 2. How is her heart?

When I ask myself this question, I am asking about her relationship with Jesus. Is she more in love with God than with any man? Is she completely sold out for the gospel? There are few things that can be difficult when you are married to someone who does not hold the same values as you do. It is literally asking for a fight on a weekly basis. I have seen so many couples at church who struggle with the fact that one or the other has no interest in being there. This causes major stress and strain on the marriage. It often leads to other issues such as unfaithfulness and divorce.

## 3. Is she Independent or Codependent?

By that I mean, is she willing to work as a team in the marriage or is it her way or the highway. I have seen many marriages fall apart because the man or the women are too independent and inflexible. They do not listen to their partner or adjust their desires to the desires of their spouse. Marriage is a team effort, not a monarchy. That is why in marriage, we must die daily to our desires so we can please the one we love, putting them above ourselves. That is true love.

There are other points I would like to add, I have one chapter to share, so that will wait until next time. Let me leave you with this, from Ephesians 5:22-33 (ESV):

*"Wives, submit to your own husbands, as to the Lord. 23 For the husband is the head of the wife even as Christ is the head of the church, his body, and is himself its Savior. Now as the church submits to Christ, so also wives should submit in e thing to their husbands. Husbands, love your wives, as*

## Chapter 7: A Man's Point of View

*Christ loved the church and gave himself up for her, that he might sanctify her, having cleansed her by the washing of water with the word, so that he might present the church to himself in splendor, without spot or wrinkle or any such thing, that she might be holy and without blemish. In the same way husbands should love their wives as their own bodies. He who loves his wife loves himself. For no one ever hated his own flesh, but nourishes and cherishes it, as Christ does the church, because we are members of his body. 'Therefore a man shall leave his father and mother and hold fast to his wife, and the two shall become one flesh.' This mystery is profound, and I am saying that it refers to Christ and the church. However, let each one of you love his wife as himself, and let the wife see that she respects her husband."*

This passage is key to my life and my marriage. Notice how amazing God is. Knowing women are smart, He only gives them two verses to obey. But for we men, knowing that we need a little more work, He gives us nine verses to live by. Then He gives us the ultimate example, telling us to love their wives as Christ loved the church. Through being the head of the household, we are serving our household.

Our wives are not housekeepers that we are free to boss around. They are our queens who we are to love as Christ loves and serves the Church. So, lady, when you find your "Mr. Right," remember this chapter. What type of woman do you want to be, and what type of man are you searching for?

Having been married to my beautiful wife for almost seven years at this point, it is clear to me that there is no better thing than to be married to your best friend. We have two amazing boys Levi and Liam, and I have seen how Melodi is a super mom to them, and the best wife I could ever ask for. Yes, I had to pursue her. But the chase was worth it. If a man is unwilling to pursue you, then he is not the man God has for you. Be patient with the Lord. Make lots of great friends, because before you know it, you may one day marry your best friend.

*Chapter 7: A Man's Point of View*

# Time to Reflect!

Question for our single ladies.

Based on the previous chapter, do you have the qualifications to become "wife material?" Yes or no. Please explain.

_____
_____
_____
_____

Question for the married ladies.

Do you submit to and support your husband? Are you a faithful woman? What is an area you believe needs improvement in your marriage?

_____
_____
_____
_____

Something to think about:

### 1 Corinthians 13:13(NIV)

*And now these three remain: faith, hope and love. But the greatest of these is love.*

### 1 Peter 4:8(NIV)

*Above all, love each other deeply, because love covers over a multitude of sins.*

### 1 Corinthians 13:7-8 (NIV)

*Love knows no limit to its endurance no end to its trust, Love still stands when all else has fallen.*

## Chapter 8:
# Breaking the Curse

*For we do not wrestle against flesh and blood, but against the rulers, against the authorities, against the cosmic powers over this present darkness, against the spiritual forces of evil in the heavenly places.*

Ephesians 6:12(NIV)

Do you know what a curse is? Today, we think of the term "cursing" as someone using foul language, profanity, or taking our Lord's name in vain. Our meaning in today's terms would be "swearing." Cursing in the Bible is not only to speak badly of someone, but evil coming upon someone. If a person is under a curse, according to the Bible, evil has come upon them in some form. It could be in the form of sickness, tragedy, or recurring bad circumstances in their lives.

Are you under a curse? Could you be? Perhaps you have experienced curses because of being disobedient to God. Curses can be the consequences of sin. It is basically an opened door or argument of the enemy (Satan) against you or your family, who seeks dominion over you. This could be a result of something done by you or by someone in your past generations. Yes, I know. This can sound scary since we have all sinned, and some have seriously sinful backgrounds.

However, you don't have to allow sin or shame paralyze you. God has given us the authority to break every curse against us in Jesus name.

The first step is for us to *recognize a curse*. To be set free and stay free we must admit there is a problem and take responsibility for it.

The second step is to *break the curse*. When we apply the blood of Jesus and the power of God's Word to our lives, all chains of bondage will be broken. Have you ever heard

## Chapter 8: Breaking the Curse

the term, "like father, like son?" As I mentioned, some curses come through our past generations (our parents, grandparents, great-grandparents), etc. Curses such as drug and alcohol use, sickness in the family, continual divorces, accidents, violence, unfaithfulness, and others.

When we give our life to Jesus, His blood removes our sin, gives us the authority to fight spiritual battles, and retake spiritual control over our lives from the enemy. We may be affected by the consequences of past generations, but Ezekiel 18:20 tells us that God *does not punish* us for the sins they committed. The effects of sin are naturally passed down from one generation to the next.

In Exodus 20:5 we find a verse that seems to contradict the passage in Ezekiel (above). It specifically states that God *does punish* successive generations for the sins of their fathers. But that refers to those children who follow in the sinful acts of their fathers (and mothers). The only one who was punished for the sins of another was Christ, who took our sins upon Himself at His crucifixion. The cure for generational curses has always been repentance.

In my family, there was a curse that passed from generations to generations. My niece was affected by it, my brother was affected by it, my grandfather, my great-grandfather, and generations before him were affected. It is a medical condition webbing the fingers or toes called *syndactyly*. Webbed fingers and toes occur when tissue connects two or more digits together. In rare cases, the fingers or toes are connected by bone. Each generation became stronger and more difficult to cure.

When I became pregnant with my son, the Lord showed me it was not a coincidence these things happened in my family. But He showed me how to pray for my son and break this generational curse once and for all. So, my husband and I began to break the bondages up to the 4$^{th}$. generation before us one-by-one removing the evil authority that caused these medical problems in the family. The first thing my husband did when our son was born was to carefully check each finger and toe. And for the glory of the Lord, he was completely normal. We made this same prayer for our nephew, Luke, who was born four months later, completely normal and healthy.

It's important for each of us to take the authority God gives us to cancel all arguments against our lives, whether it is a sickness, bad habits, poverty, etc. The blood of Jesus Christ has the power to destroy the evil dominion over you and your next generation. The Prophet Nehemiah provides an example for us. When he returned to find Jerusalem in ruins, he repented to God for sins of Israel. He was not guilty, but he repented in their place.

It is important to ask The Lord for a sincere heart, one that regrets every sinful act of immorality, rebellion, deceit, abuse, occultism, witchcraft, idolatry, and others alike. When we choose to genuinely repent, we receive God's forgiveness. The enemy loves to cause us grief when

## Chapter 8: Breaking the Curse

there are sins connected to our lives, personal or generational for which we haven't repented nor confessed. Please understand this is not a prayer that you can simply repeat in your head. It is important that you confess with your voice. Make sure that you are truly repentant as you confess these sins. Otherwise, the confession means little.

It is important that you are repentant on behalf of your family as well. If you continue to be angry and bitter towards your family, your prayers will be ineffective. Ask God to give you a spirit of forgiveness. After you have confessed all sins, renounce and cancel any claims of Satan upon your life in the name of Jesus Christ. Tell the Lord you are thankful for showing you the great power that there is in the blood of Jesus because through it, your entire life has been changed. All the generational curses that have affected you have been broken by the power of His blood.

I encourage you to spend some time in worship and praise to the Lord. Thank him in advance for deliverance and healing that He is going to bring into your life. Above all, believe that the Lord will free you and your future generations.

Remember what the Bible says in John 10:10: *"The thief comes only to steal and kill and destroy; I have come that they may have life and have it to the full."* Stay close to the Lord in prayer. Read His Word so you can stand firm and fortified against the attacks of the enemy. Keep your eyes on the Lord. The Lord loves you and He is forever faithful.

# Time to Reflect!

Can you think of any curses in your life? Are you able to recognize generational patterns within your family?

*And the prayer offered in faith will make the sick person well; the Lord will raise them up. If they have sinned, they will be forgiven. Therefore, confess your sins to each other and pray for each other so that you may be healed. The prayer of a righteous person is powerful and effective*

James 5:15-16 (NIV).

Take a moment to analyze what you read, prepare yourself to pray in your secret place. Talk to Him, confess to Him, and truly repent of all your sins. And believe God will bring you to victory. The moment you do this, Satan will lose all authority over you in Jesus name!

## Chapter 9:
# Tears Turned into Dancing

*You have turned for me my mourning into dancing; You have put off my sackcloth and clothed me with gladness, To the end that my glory may sing praise to You and not be silent. O Lord my God, I will give thanks to you forever!*

Psalms 30:11-12 (NIV)

## Beauty, Strength, & Power

Have you ever been hurt? Have you been lied to, mistreated and or neglected? This chapter is for those who haven't had it easy in life. For those who suffered and maybe never had a chance to truly break free from it all. Perhaps it has been a while since you have talked about that sad chapter of your life, but there are certain subjects at times, that remind you of it all.

The Bible verse at the beginning of this chapter is one of my favorite Bible promises. God turns our tears into dancing! He replaces our sadness with gladness. However, notice He does not necessarily stop our pain or make it disappear, No! He transforms it into everlasting joy! He takes our failure and creates success. God is so merciful to us. As the Apostle Paul wrote: *"All things work together for good to them that love Him and to those who are the called according to His purpose"* Romans 8:28(NIV).

A few years ago, some of the leaders of our church attended a convention in Los Angeles, where we all received something special from God. In this conference the preacher challenged us to begin to pray according to His will. To expect the impossible if we simply believed in Him. They challenged each person at the convention to go out into the city of Los Angeles and pray for every person who crossed our path. It was amazing to see our faith come alive and experience miracles occur left and right through the streets of LA.

Our goal was not only to show people what God can

## Chapter 9: Tears Turned Into Dancing

do for them, but to also share the gospel, the good news of salvation through Jesus Christ, to each of them. I could not believe my eyes! The Spirit of the Lord was there so powerfully. We saw people who had never heard the gospel experience miracle healing in their sight, ability to hear restored, broken legs healed, and more. As healing came, we led many of them to receive Christ as their Savior. That day, as hundreds of people in Los Angeles received Jesus as their Lord and savior, I felt so on fire for God, and excited to see what He would do next. Along with of our leadership team we agreed to take this great movement back to our church. Sunday morning service came around, His presence remained with us.

That morning our eyes were drawn to a young girl in a wheelchair, and we were burdened to pray for her. When the service finished, we approached her and asked if we could pray for her. In response, she told us that many others had prayed for her with no result in the past. Still, she allowed us to pray for her once more. She explained that she was born with a condition called Cerebral Palsy, which is a congenital disorder of movement, muscle tone, or posture.

We began to cry out to the Lord for a miracle. When we finished, however, we noticed that nothing had happened. We prayed again, and again, and again. Then a silence came over the room.

I asked, "Do you believe God can heal you?"

She responded, "I think so, but to be honest, I'm

afraid."

We realize that it wasn't that God would not heal her, but the fear she had carried all these years was stronger than her faith.

At that moment, we changed our prayers. We asked the Lord to remove the spirit of unbelief, break the curse of fear, and bring total healing to her heart. That is when the miracle occurred. Joy came over her and she began to cry tears of happiness and sing to the Lord. Instantly clothed in faith, expecting to receive her miracle, her dormant muscles and weak bones were strengthened, paralysis left, and stood and walked.

Maybe you are not physically paralyzed, but inside, you desperately need a miracle. Here's the problem. We have become experts at faking we are "alright." But if anyone could see us from the inside they would see that we are wounded, we feel abandoned, we are paralyzed with fear and incapable of asking for help. My dear friends, this must stop today! Open your heart to the Lord, give him every one of your sorrows, repent from your sins, every tragedy, and any type of pain in your heart. As you read this page, the Spirit of the Lord is with you. He has been longing to have a real conversation with you. He wants to mend what has been broken and make it into something new. Now is the moment to speak up, let God remove the weight from your shoulders once and for all.

Let's take time to dwell on this promise. Our sorrows,

## Chapter 9: Tears Turned Into Dancing

tragedies, and failures are real. We don't deny that. But they are also "raw material" for a divine transformation that our Lord will perform in His time for His glory. And we too *will dance!* God will do it. Our part is simply to believe, wait, and hold tightly to this wonderful promise! Although the consequences of our sins (including sexually immorality, unplanned pregnancies, diseases, and emotional ties, etc.) linger, Jesus will forgive and cleanse us and give us wisdom for each issue. He gives us the opportunity to start over and rebuild our lives. It's essential that we take the necessary steps toward our restoration.

*Humility is the first step* in our spiritual and emotional restoration. To start the process, we must recognize our nothingness before our Almighty God. Scripture teaches us in 2 Chronicles 7:14:

*If my people, which are called by my name, shall humble themselves, and pray, and seek my face, and turn from their wicked ways; then will I hear from heaven, and will forgive their sin, and will heal their land.*

*Prayer is the second step* in our spiritual restoration. It is an act of humility. Prayer is *not* to present God with a list of our desires. God *cares* about our needs and He instructs us to *"cast all our cares on Him"* (1 Peter 5:7).

*Communion with God is the third step* in our spiritual restoration. It is to seek God's face. It means to draw near to Him, to live in His presence, and to fellowship with Him. Prayer is the door through which we enter into communion with God. It is a conversation with Him, not a monologue. It is to be intimate with Him as if we were literally face-to-face with Him.

Repentance for believers is described in Romans 12:2 as transformation by a renewing of our minds. This happens as we allow the thoughts of God and who He is to replace our doubts and negative memories.

*Chapter 9: Tears Turned Into Dancing*

# Time to Reflect!

A Bible verse to remember.

*I cried to him with my mouth, and high praise was on my tongue. If I had cherished iniquity in my heart, the Lord would not have listened. But truly God has listened; he has attended to the voice of my prayer. Blessed be God, because he has not rejected my prayer or removed his steadfast love from me!* Psalms 66:17-20 (NIV)

2) Will you be brave today? Write a list of things that once paralyzed your faith, your hope and dreams.

_____

_____

_____

_____

3) Let's declare this prayer in faith

*Heavenly Father, I let go of all the emotional, spiritual, and physical paralysis. I receive your healing. I am filled with your never-ending love and joy in the name of Jesus Christ. Amen!*

# Chapter 10:
# Gift of Motherhood

*Behold, children are a heritage from the Lord, the fruit of the womb a reward.*

Psalm 127:3 (NIV)

**It** was a beautiful Friday afternoon in the month of June 2014 when I found out I was expecting a baby. I was sitting at my desk waiting to get off of work, experiencing a few pregnancy symptoms, when I decided to take a pregnancy test. The moment I looked at the results I began to cry and thank God for my unexpected miracle.

At that very moment I consecrated my baby to the Lord. I told God that my child, whether a boy or a girl, would be my offering to Him. I asked Him to teach me how to be a mother, according to His heart, someone who would protect, provide, guide and love without limits. I promised that I would prepare my baby to become a man or woman of God, a warrior, someone who would use every skill and talent to serve Him.

That same afternoon I rushed home to tell my husband that we were expecting! It was the best feeling to tell the one I love that we were going to have a baby. His reaction was priceless! After I told him, he stayed silent for what felt like an eternity. Then he said, "I need to buy a family car." He embraced me and together we began to plan our future of new little bundle of joy. As time went by, as a new mom, I experienced different emotions, excitement and insecurity at the same time. I had many questions and was determined to be the best mom I could be, but I didn't know how.

Interestingly, I had not always been so excited about becoming a mom. Throughout my teen years, I did not want a child. Society had convinced me that I wasn't fit for the job. The emphasis was placed on becoming a successful woman, rather than a successful mom. I was advised about the terrible responsibility of parenthood: childbirth pain, loss of freedom, sleepless nights, delay on career opportunities, loss of power and the dreaded dependence on men.

But those were nothing but pessimistic views of selfish people who were ignorant about the joy of being a mother, the love and laughter, purpose and meaning it brings to your life. It was the enemy's way to steel the wonderful opportunity of motherhood. As I developed a closer relationship with God, He showed me that the most influential women in history were moms. Children come with great challenges as well as great rewards and mothers leave a legacy in the world.

When I met my husband, I found the true meaning of love and I opened the door of my heart to be forever his and become the mother of his children. God used John to show me that real love in a marriage isn't temporary, but it should last a lifetime. The fruit of our love would bring unity between us forever.

I did not know this then, but to become a mother would be the most profound and unique adventure of my life. Motherhood is an experience unlike any other on earth. There is nothing as profound, nothing that will stretch you so far beyond anything you previously imagined. It is remarkably challenging, and uniquely rewarding at the same time. Other life experiences may bring you joy or fulfillment, or encourage you to grow, but none is on the same scale as becoming a mother.

Nine months later, on Friday evening after our youth service, I began to feel anxious, tired and mostly hungry. So, I begged a lady at church, our main intercessor, to pray for me to have the baby soon! Sure enough, I went to bed and I started to feel an excitement in my tummy, butterflies which also felt like light cramps. I said to my husband "John, I think things are starting to happen." A couple of hours later, while sleeping my water broke! And yes, I panicked! I have never seen my legs shake so much!

John rushed me to the hospital, where after 23 hours of labor on April 5th, 2015 our baby boy Levi Maverick Lein was born! Levi brought so much joy to our family that night. My husband and I, the new grandparents, aunts, and uncles were filled with joy and excitement to welcome the newest member of our family to the world. The first little smile, the first tears shed, and the first baby laugh surely captured our hearts, and created our most beautiful and unforgettable memories. Childbirth wasn't easy, but it is surely one of life's most rewarding events.

I fell in love with this Bible verse speaking about of being that woman and mother God created us to be.

*She is clothed with strength and dignity; she can laugh at the days to come. She speaks with wisdom, and faithful instruction is on her tongue. She watches over the affairs of*

## Chapter 10: Gift of Motherhood

*her household and does not eat the bread of idleness. Her children arise and call her blessed; her husband also, and he praises her: 'Many women do noble things, but you surpass them all.'* Proverbs 31:25-29 (NIV)

To become a parent is truly a gift from God. Today, I encourage every woman to take the opportunity to see the beauty of having and raising children. Invite God to lead you in your decisions. He will provide the perfect husband and the best father for your children. Trust God. His plans are far greater than ours.

Beauty, Strength, & Power

# Time to Reflect!

1. In a few words, describe your experience as a child. And how this marked your life.

_____
_____
_____
_____

2. Whether you have children or not. What is your greatest fear/insecurity when you think of your future generation?

_____
_____
_____
_____

## Chapter 11:
# Precious Cargo

*Every good and perfect gift is from above, coming down from the Father of the heavenly lights, who does not change like shifting shadows* James 1:17 (NIV).

***God Did It Again!*** Our second miracle is on the way. Dear friend, this is a chapter I never intended to write. But here I am writing it, with tears in my eyes, and a lump in my throat. And my hands feel shaky at these keys. *I'm pregnant again.* God has done it once more.

A year after our son Levi was born, I began to ask the Lord for another child. My husband and I began to pray and plan for our second baby. Months passed and there were no results. I questioned if I would even be able to conceive another child.

The enemy filled my mind with thoughts of infertility. I became a broken woman, angry and confused. In my mind, I believed once pregnant with my first child, I had control over every decision to conceive a second and possibly third child. Boy was I wrong! During that year, I learned that everything works according to God's timing and not ours. Pastor Cesar Castellanos, my pastor and mentor once told me, "A wise person always prays according to God's will. For He has perfected the blue prints of our lives, even before we were born." All we must to do is to lean not in our own understanding but to trust in Him with all of our heart, all of our mind and all of our soul.

As I write this, our son Levi is now two-years-old. The past two years have been amazing, we have learned so much about this little person God has placed in our care. I've watched him grow out of his tiny newborn clothes into his little boy clothes. He looks older by the minute. We prayed that God would give us more children. Even though we were already beyond blessed to have even one beautiful child. Many people do not get this opportunity.

In 2016, God gave me a specific word as I prepared my message to share at our Braveheart Convention here at Evermore Church. Ironically the topic given to me by my mother-in-law and senior pastor was, "Mother of Multitudes." I thought for sure God was trying to teach me something.

The Lord gave me this Bible verse "I will make you fruitful; I will make nations of you, and kings will come from you. I will establish my covenant as an everlasting covenant between me and you and your descendants after you for the generations to come, to be your God and the God of your descendants after you" Genesis 17:6-7(NIV)

This word struck my heart. Earlier that year John and I initiated the English ministry of Evermore Church. This was a miracle, my husband and I prayed for this for many years. God opened the doors and made a way. Finally, I began my journey in becoming a pastor and spiritual mother to many. That day at the convention, as I began to share this word, God showed me He was going to give me a child. In the same way as He opened the doors for our church and gave the opportunity to become a mother of multitudes, He was going to bless our lives with a baby very soon. I remember crying before His presence in gratitude of God's immense love for me. Exactly two weeks later, once again I started feeling pregnancy symptoms, so I rushed to the store to purchase a pregnancy test. To my amazement, I was six-weeks pregnant, which meant that I was already pregnant at the time the Lord gave me the word at the women's convention. God had already blessed me with another child and was simply testing my faith to believe His promises are "yes" and "amen".

A week later I was rushed to the hospital due to some bleeding. Immediately I was taken to be tested. The doctors didn't know what was causing the bleeding, but suspected I was experiencing a possible miscarriage. Again, my faith was being tested. As I waited for the results in that cold emergency room alone, it seemed that the room filled with darkness. I felt as if I were surrounded by shadows, filling my mind with fear, anxiety, and doubt.

I closed my eyes and for a moment began to visualize Jesus standing before me. I pro- claimed the blood of Jesus over my baby's life. I rebuked the spirit of fear and canceled the decree of death upon my baby. I immediately felt the shadow flee, and in a matter of seconds, an over- whelming peace came upon me. I was reminded of God's promise to me and declared Christ's victory over our lives. A couple of hours later the doctors came back with the good news. Our baby was strong and healthy, and I was nine-weeks pregnant.

Again, God had mercy on me and reminded me that He is forever faithful. We were expecting another boy! My husband and I decided to name our son *Liam Nixon Lein*.

## Chapter 11: Precious Cargo

Liam means "determined guardian, my people, and unwavering protector." Nixon means "triumphant/victorious people, strong and courageous." I absolutely love his name.

As I write this chapter, I am 40-weeks pregnant. I can't wait to hold him. My heart is full of joy and gratitude to God who has blessed me with another child.

In July 28, 2017, Liam Nixon Lein was born. He is perfect! I was beyond blessed, because he was healthy, and one ounce short of eight pounds. The delivery was a complete success, it fast and without complications, praise the Lord! I thank God for this every morning I wake up and see his precious face. I don't have a life to myself anymore. I do not have time to style my hair, get my nails done, or even go to the bathroom alone (sorry, too much information). Eight hours of sleep is completely out the question and eating has become an exhausting marathon. For those who have small children you know exactly what I am talking about. For those who are not there yet, brace yourselves, it's coming... But that is what being a mom is all about.

That is why God gave us women this important job. He knows we are the only ones capable of doing it gracefully, yet with so much strength. We dedicate our entire lives to serve them and make sure they are well taken care of. It's a *selfless love*. Being a mother is one of the hardest, yet most rewarding jobs there is. It takes some getting used to, but I wouldn't trade it for the world! I am privileged now to be a stay-at-home mom and full-time pastor. My heart is full!

Of course, my parents in law would like for us to have a third baby... Bless their heart. But I am content with my two boys. The future is absolutely in God's hands. *"'For I know the plans I have for you,' declares the LORD, 'plans to prosper you and not to harm you, plans to give you hope and a future'"* Jeremiah 29:11(NIV).

*Chapter 11: Precious Cargo*

# Time to Reflect!

How many kids do you plan to have? If you already have kids Do you want more? Describe what being a mother means or would mean to you.

_____

_____

_____

_____

_____

     Remember, whether you are a mother or not you are more than capable for the job. You will be an example to your children and generations to come. So make it count! Be that excellent woman of God, an excellent wife, and a loving protectant mother as the woman described in Proverb 31:10-31. The world depends on it.

## Chapter 12:
# Construct Your Future

*For this reason, He is the mediator of a new covenant, so that, since a death has taken place for the redemption of the transgressions that were committed under the first covenant, those who have been called may receive the promise of the eternal inheritance.* Hebrews 9:159(NIV)

## Beauty, Strength, & Power

Have you ever watched a relay race? If so, then you know how important it is to carefully pass the baton smoothly the next runner. In fact, to be able to pass the baton correctly is as important as running fast. There is a perfect example of this from the 1996 Olympics.

The United States had been the favorite quarter-mile relay team in almost every Olympic competition. The U.S won 14 of the previous 18 Olympic quarter-mile relays. We always placed four of the fastest sprinters in the country to represent us on the track. But unfortunately, in 1996, the U.S. team lost to the Canadian team.

Why did our amazing group of U.S. sprinters lose? They were disqualified because of an inability to properly pass the baton from one runner to the next. You might wonder why I offer this analogy. I do so to introduce the topic of our preparing to hand off the baton to the next generation. If we are careless about principles and morals we pass down, we may cause our future generation to become weak minded, sinful and cursed.

The Bible compares the Christian life to a race. Hebrews 12:1 (NKJV) says, *"Therefore we also, since we are surrounded by so great a cloud of witnesses, let us lay aside every weight, and the sin which so easily ensnares us, and let us run with endurance the race that is set before us."* Life is a relay race! God is not only concerned about how well we run. He also cares about those runners who will come after us, who will take our baton and run the next lap? Our children are the next generation of runners.

As parents, we worry about our children, what kind of people they will become, and how well will they interact with others. Not only when they are young, but when they become adults. What kind of example are we leaving them? What is the greatest thing they will inherit from us? Families often try to encourage moral values and to leave a physical inheritance for their children.

Unfortunately, our plans do not always work out. The word of God teaches us; naked we come to this earth and naked we shall leave. Meaning nothing lasts forever, all material things will fade away.

Today I want to offer you something more, something that will never vanish; this will transform your generation in a positive way. It is the love of God through His son Jesus that gives us true love, freedom, and power. God provides strength and authority to remove curses from our lives and replace these with His eternal blessings. There is no better possession we can pass down to our children than the Father's love. This is the greatest and richest inheritance.

There is nothing more valuable to me than to provide my children the greatest gift ever given to me. It is the gift of eternal life that comes from our Lord Jesus Christ. From the day I was born, my parents showed me His everlasting love. Every life lesson was based on the Word of God. I have the amazing blessing of having parents who are pastors. They taught me that God is always faithful; in the good times and the bad, in sickness and in health, in times of abundance and times of scarcity. This is the foundation of my life, my marriage, and my future generation.

Honestly, my family is not perfect, no one's is. Even though we are a priestly family, we have gone through very tough situations such as a death in the family, miscarriage, serious health problems, divorce, financial and emotional struggles and more. This book is not about how perfect and easy life is when you encounter God. But it is to magnify God even when things become difficult and hard to bear. To glorify Him even when life's storms seem to nearly drown you. It is to trust in Him when things seem to be falling apart. To believe that He loves us, no matter what. The purpose is to allow Him to transform our greatest weaknesses into our greatest strengths.

I believe the only reason God has allowed me to become a mother and a pastor; it is to disciple my children and anyone willing to listen to me about the grace of God. Our heavenly Father cares for his children, He constantly watches over us. He is immensely kind and generous. He will never abandon you nor forsake you. His love for you is unlimited and His plan for you is to bless you abundantly. He wants to fill you with joy and give you the assurance that everything is under His control. Nothing compares to knowing this truth. My friend, the greatest inheritance you can leave to your children is the privilege to know Jesus Christ and to accept Him as their personal Lord and Savior.

*Chapter 12: Construct Your Future*

# Time to Reflect!

1. If God decides to take you with Him this year, this month, or even today. Are you saved? Are you ready to go with Him?

   _____

2. Based on your previous answer, what will be left once you are gone?

   _____

   _____

   _____

3. How will people remember you? Once you are gone, what is your inheritance here on the earth?

   _____

   _____

   _____

   _____

I invite you to make this prayer with me.

*Lord, today I surrender all that I am and all I have to you. I ask You to forgive my sins. Wash me clean by the blood of Jesus Christ. Remove any curse on my life and place divine favor and your blessing upon me. Father give me your identity and allow me to take part in your inheritance. Make my path straight so that future generations may see you in me. I want to become successful in my walk with you, my testimony and become a blessing in all areas of my life. I declare the mark of God is upon me and I leave my footprints on this earth as a true woman of God. Amen!*

# Grand Finale
# (Bonus Chapter)

*Your beauty should not come from outward adornment, such as elaborate hairstyles and the wearing of gold jewelry or fine clothes. Rather, it should be that of your inner self, the unfading beauty of a gentle and quiet spirit, which is of great worth in God's sight.* 1 Peter 3:3-4(NIV)

## Beauty, Strength, & Power

Have you ever allowed negative thoughts to creep in— thoughts like, "I am not good enough; I am not pretty enough; or, "I am not smart enough?" Frankly, I have, more times than I would like to admit. It is easy to lose hope in these situations and to feel like it would be easier to give up. However, I would like to tell you something important, you are a daughter of the highest King. You have been created in the likeness of the most beautiful, and perfect being, God Himself. You, my darling, are a LIMITLESS woman!

This was the main topic of our women's *2017 Braveheart Convention* here at Evermore Church. I was privileged and honored to open the conference speaking about the abundant love and worth God has given each of us. I shared how God instructs us to become limitless people. Although sometimes there are certain limitations that come from God. He created certain rules for our own good, limitations that separate good and evil. These limits are designed for our own protection.

When we began to dream and prepare for this women's conference, God revealed the name "Limitless" to the pastor and founder of *Braveheart* Jeannie Lein and led her to this Scripture: *"Enlarge the place of your tent, stretch your tent curtains wide, do not limit yourself; lengthen your cords, strengthen your stakes"* Isaiah 54:4(NIV)

In this verse, we begin to understand that God's plan for you and I, is for us to expand, to grow, and to succeed. Unfortunately, there are other types of limitations that we sometimes allow in our lives. Limitations we ourselves create or allow others to contaminate us with negativism. This includes things like; character flaws, financial struggle, physical limitations, emotional trauma, spiritual barriers, etc.

Perhaps until now, you have been completely oblivious about this. But my prayer is that in the next few minutes God may reveal these "limitations" in your life and will transform your weaknesses into strengths that you may become truly limitless!

You may be asking, "What does being a limitless woman really mean?" Well, to answer that question, I have given each letter to the word "limitless" a meaning. These are the following:

**L** is for *loyalty*. To be limitless, we must be loyal. This means to be faithful to God, to our husbands (if you are married), or to your future husband. Loyalty must be your identity.

**I** stands for *integrity*. To be honest, and have strong moral principles is a virtue. The true meaning of simplicity, sincerity, truthfulness, and righteousness.

**M** is for *motivated*. A motivated woman shows interest and enthusiasm in all that she does.

From the moment we wake up, we choose to make it a good day. Your attitude determines the outcome of every situation.

**I**, stands for *intelligent*. An intelligent woman is wise and fully aware of her thoughts and actions. By the way this is not always easy to do. She carefully weighs and balances her daily decisions.

**T** stands for *talented*. God has created you with specific talents, it is a shame to keep them hidden. I encourage you to develop and use yours to grow in life and bless others. Using God's gifts to serve Him is the best use of them. Do not procrastinate anymore! Take full advantage of your God given gifts!

**L** is for *leader*. There are two kinds of people in the world, followers and leaders. You are a natural born leader. As godly women, we should become an example and have the ability to guide others with divine direction. I encourage you to become a leader in your home, in your job, and in your ministry. Because if you do not lead, someone else will.

**E** is for *edified*. To be edified is to be instructed and encouraged in moral, intellectual, and spiritual things. I encourage you to start spending time with daily devotional, private moments with God. You will be ministered to, disciplined and instructed when you spend intimate time with God. This is where you will find the answers to every important decision.

**S** stands for *strong*. Whoever said "women are weak" never gave birth to a baby! We women are not weak. In fact, we were created to handle life's pressure and to remain strong in any circumstance. Yes, we go through many trials and extremely tough situations. But this is when we rise and keep on fighting. Because even when the enemy attacks and there is no one left to rely on, God gives us strength and power to conquer and emerge victoriously!

**S**, our final "S," stands for *successful*. We were each created to accomplish our God-given purpose. Failing is not an option for a *limitless woman*. Are you a mother, a business woman, or an entrepreneur? Whatever your title may be, do everything with excellence. Success is part of your identity.

God is leading me to tell you, for those of you who have been directed by Him to start a project, a career or a company you must complete it. Do not give up, keep working at it until you have fulfilled that dream. His dreams and plans for you are to prosper you and not to harm you to give you hope and a future.

My darling, you are beautiful, strong, brave and powerful. Through prayer, the Lord will reveal the hindrances that have restricted you from achieving your dreams and caused you to yield to your own perceived limitations. He will transform you into a woman who is limitless and will cause you to fulfill His purpose. The Lord will guide you to reach your goals and fulfill your purpose here on earth. God approves of you. He has chosen you. You are absolutely qualified to be triumphant. Never allow the enemy to tell you otherwise. You are limitless because your heavenly Father is limitless!

Beauty, Strength, & Power

# Time to Reflect!

What do you believe has been the greatest limitation in your life?

_____

_____

Let's dream a little... If you had the chance to become whatever you wanted in life, what would it be?

_____

_____

In faith, what is your goal this year?

_____

_____

What do you wish to accomplish in the next five years?

_____

_____

*Grand Finale (Bonus Chapter)*

What is your greatest aspiration in the next ten years?

_____
_____
_____

# Contact the Author

Melodi Lein
2059 Atlanta Ave
Riverside, CA 92507
(909) 742-2494

www.melodilein.com
Email: melodilein@me.com

Personal Instagram: melodilein
www.instagram.com/melodilein

Beauty & Fitness: beauty_strength_ power
www.instagram.com/beauty_strength_power

Facebook: www.facebook.com/melodilein

Evermore Church website: www.evermorechurch.org

Evermore Church Instagram: evermorechurchee
www.instagram.com/evermorechurchee

www.ingramcontent.com/pod-product-compliance
Lightning Source LLC
Chambersburg PA
CBHW052101070526
44584CB00017B/2279